A New Attitude

A New Attitude

First published by Griffin Lore, 2023

Typesetting and cover design by The Book Typesetters
hello@thebooktypesetters.com
07422 598 168
www.thebooktypesetters.com

The moral right of the author has been asserted.

ISBN 978-1-7394306-0-3

A New Attitude

Verses for everyday life

Chris Griffin

This book is dedicated
to all those who are brave enough to
contemplate changing their attitude
towards their life, loves and relationships.

Ways to read this book

I usually only reflected on and wrote one verse in a day, so why not read and reflect on just one verse per day?

Open the book randomly and read a verse.

Scan the index and select a title that catches your eye.

Never feel obliged to read the whole book front to back. This was never my intention for the reader.

Read only what you enjoy or what intrigues you.

Dip in and out at will.

Or, any other way that suits you.

Contents

Introduction   9
The Thread weaving throughout this book of verse

Love & Loss   11
Can you ever have one without risking the other?

Equity & Equality   27
Cue: Oh no, not that old chestnut again!

To Plan or Not?   47
That is a very good question indeed!

What I Have Learnt   67
through life's ups and downs

Exploring Our Dark Side   87
Fears, doubts, shame and guilt

A New Way of Living   111
Reminders of what makes life easier

About the Author   129

Acknowledgements   130

Index   131

Introduction

The Thread weaving throughout this book of verse

It is my belief that we all have both feminine and masculine attributes within us, though the balance between the two will be unique to each individual.

Unfortunately, the terms masculine and feminine risk conjuring up the vision of gender, so leading many to believe that they are wholly masculine because of their male gender or wholly feminine because of their female gender.

For that reason, some will have difficulty accessing their masculine side and others their feminine side and would express surprise that they might have the choice to do so. Even fearing that to do so would somehow dilute their maleness or femaleness.

But, if we deny our full selves, in other words, our unique combination of being both masculine and feminine, to some degree at the same time, we end up denying ourselves.

This book is about contemplating the value of recognising both the masculine and the feminine in both ourselves and others; something I was compelled to explore during a time of great upheaval in my own life.

It also reflects on how the feminine is currently deemed to be of less significance in many societies, so making it harder for all of us to find, respect and embrace our feminine attributes.

Love & Loss

Can you ever have one without risking the other?

The Very Best Gift

You encapsulate
The best thing that ever happened to me
And the very worst thing too.
In a nutshell
You awoke my heart
And then rode roughshod over it!
I was too young to stand alone.

But ultimately, you led me to find myself
To be myself, come what may.

So, perversely, you gave me the very best gift
The gift of self-love.
A love that can never be taken from me
A love that brings me great happiness
Each and every single day.

Loss

Can you remember the past without longing
Remember it fondly
With no feeling of loss?

It happened, so can't be undone.
It must be let go though
If life is to go on
As a wonderful, exciting adventure
As a life that fulfils its potential.

Be brave and reopen your heart to love.
It's love that makes the world go round
Don't let it stop it in its tracks.

I Don't Really Like You!

I don't particularly like much about you!
I don't like the choices you have made
The lifestyle you lead
The priorities you have.

But it seems that none of this matters.
No-one has touched my heart as you once did
Not before or after.
My love endures, even if my liking does not.

Love & Loss

To love means running the risk of loss.

Loss means running the risk of loving again
Choosing to live half a life
Or to live a full life, right to the end.

Grief serves a necessary purpose
It processes loss so we can find completion
Ready to move forward once more.

It is the moving forward that life is about.

Longing

Longing for something, for someone
Preoccupies the mind
Excludes reality
In favour of a made-up world
A world where such longing is requited.

It uses up energy
Takes up valuable bandwidth
Leaves so much less for the rest of life.

It is the rest of life that is real.
The longing is just
Wishful thinking
A waste of energy
Of bandwidth
Of life.

Player

A player is charismatic and charming, a ladies' man
Magnetic in their attraction.
But have no mistake
They know it and hone their skills.

A player is fearful
Fearful of being overwhelmed
By their feelings.
Fearful of commitment
Of losing their freedom
Of being beholden in any shape or form
To another.
A player needs to be in charge.
All this they are far less likely
To admit to themselves
To acknowledge that they might be fearful
Is a step too far.

No. Ignore the fact of fear!
Repeat the same damaging patterns
The same broken promises
Just more notches on the bedpost.
Life is too exciting to be limited
Limited by responsibility to another
Isn't it?

There is no end of willing partners
Each believing that they can be the one
To tame that freedom
Each doomed to fail…

But even a player can change their ways.
It takes time and effort
A loss of something to gain something better
An acceptance of compromise.
Only time will tell
If they are committed enough to succeed.

So, heed the red flags
Be circumspect
Watch and wait
Be ready to sever ties.
But also, be ready to acknowledge
Change if it happens.

Whoever takes on a player
Must be strong in themselves
As strong as that player.
Strong enough to walk away
To know if fingers are about to get burned
And to act accordingly
Without regret for what could never have been.

An Idea of Me

You loved an idea of me.
A me that complemented your lifestyle.
My looks, my behaviour, my likes, my dislikes
All dictated and guided by you.

But that was not the real me
It could not be sustained
Without losing the real me.
The real me that irritated you
Beyond measure.

So, did you love me?
No
And that truth is bitter to swallow.
But swallow it I must
If I am to be true to myself
To love myself as I deserve to be loved.

Touch

It is the lightest of touches
That draws the attention
That soothes
And of which you want so much more.

It does not intrude
But still makes its mark
By promising much
And letting imagination
Fill in the gaps.

Mistaken Identity

Grieving loss, it is unavoidable grief.
We may be glorious energetic beings
But we have human emotions
And human heartbreak.

Recovery.
It is a long, lonely road
But there is always an end
Though seemingly endless at the time.

Emerging at last
From that long, interminable tunnel
Refreshed, reinvigorated
Never thought I'd feel this way again.
Relief
A so welcome respite
Long may it last!

Getting on with life, happy, joyful
Then BAM!...   Slipping back.
Old patterns of loss, heartbreak pushing through
Puncturing contentment, peace of mind.
Why?
How much more resolution
Could possibly be needed to fully move on?
Despair.
Will I ever, ever get over it, however hard I try?

Then a strange
But very compelling insight arises
What if it is not my energy
Mine to resolve?
Such close, energetic, empathic connections
Do not just simply disappear
When we physically part
We have to work at it
Work at truly letting go.
But it takes two to fully break
That particular energetic bond.
What if, just if
I am mistaking these recurring, distressing emotions
As my own, when they are not?

What if I am still allowing our past, deep connection
To so endure that I am once again
Not noticing where I end and the other begins?

How to deal with that?
Perhaps my boundaries have been misplaced
Keeping others at bay whilst still allowing
The chaotic, mixed, confused emotions of the other
Free access to my heart
To then be misidentified as my own.

It explains so much!
I have done good work; I have moved on.

It is the other
Who has not found the bravery yet
To dig deep enough
To let go energetically as well as physically.

Remind yourself
It is over
You have learnt from the experience
You are reborn
You cannot help another through that same journey
However much you want to.

So, keep on repeating this reminder to yourself
As often as is necessary
'Not my circus, not my monkeys',
Then get on with your day, your life
No regrets necessary.

Loyalty

If to be loyal to you
Requires me to be disloyal to myself
Which loyalty is more important?

Does choosing myself make me selfish
Trigger my guilt
Prove me unworthy?

But does choosing you
Cause my life to be less so
To be unfulfilled?
Does it require sacrifice on my part
Make me a victim?

Why should anyone offer themselves as a sacrifice?
Why should anyone remain unfulfilled?
Why should anyone have to be a victim?

No, it is a tough choice
But the choice is clear.
Choose myself first
My first loyalty is to me
To achieve my own success and fulfilment
To be happy and content.

No guilt required.

Equity & Equality

Cue: Oh no, not that old chestnut again!

I Have a Question

We talk about being emasculated
As being something that is most undesirable.
It describes what happens to a male being deprived
Of their masculinity and masculine traits.

We rarely talk about being defeminated
As being something that is equally undesirable.
It happens to a female being similarly deprived
Of their femininity and feminine traits.

Why the discrepancy, I wonder?
Does it bear scrutiny and a redress of balance
If equity is to be a serious ambition?

I Will Never Be a Feminist!

I am not a feminist
I am a powerful Feminine.
Why do we need feminists?
We don't have need for a masculinist.

If a feminist is a female who strives for equality
So far so good, it is fair to say.
It is, though, far better to be more ambitious
By aiming for equity instead.

To be a feminist implies that there is a need
For a Feminine to take up a fight for their rights.
That it is not sufficient to simply expect
To be treated as equals
No fight being called for or necessary.
To be denied equity is undeniably unacceptable
The result of ignorant behaviour.
It is shameful, a perversion of justice
It is as simple as that.
No fight is needed in order to simply expose
Inequity for exactly what it is.

A feminist is a magnet for masculine ridicule.
So, is it Masculines who create a need for a feminist
Whose behaviour is easier to dismiss?

And being tempted to fight
Risks pulling Feminines into
Playing Masculines at masculine games.
It pulls them into the masculine arena
The arena of fighting and combat.

But Feminines are not combative
They do not need to fight fights.
They simply require equity
And why not?

So, shame bad behaviour, expose inequity
Refuse to engage when respect is not offered.
Talk and write about injustice
Reveal it for what it is.

Be proud to be feminine, it is after all
Your right to be exactly who you are.
Stand strong, be powerful, do not feel obliged
To be an oh so conveniently weaponised feminist.

Why live in a skin dictated by others
When you can be comfortable in
What is your own most feminine not feminist skin?

Equity

What do we mean by equity?
Is equity all about helping others
To all behave the same?
To ensure that all have the same opportunities
So enabling all to fit in
With our existing norms
Existing systems, existing society?

Or, is it about respecting
And valuing and addressing
Our differences, all in equal measure?

The first is equality and is simpler to implement
To tick the equality box so to speak.
The other is equity and far, far more challenging
Requiring, I dare to suggest
A long overdue paradigm shift!
A paradigm shift.
'Why?' You might ask.

Because our norms, systems and societies
Have evolved over a very long period of time.
It is beliefs, long established, that dictate and guide
What is acceptable and what is not.
To question such beliefs is no easy task
As protocol is not on our side.

But for true equity to fully emerge
We must question all our beliefs
So that beliefs that no longer serve
May be challenged.
It is tough, it is profound
It takes bravery and determination.

Why bother
When things, for you, are okay, why bother?

Because our tolerance that 'I'm alright, Jack'
Makes the status quo perfectly okay
Prolongs the deeply embedded inequity
That causes others so much everyday grief.

To change the norms, systems and society
Requires a majority consensus.
If the 'I'm alright, Jacks' support what exists
Nothing will ever change.

So, if you have doubts but can't be bothered
Because you, yourself, are alright
Well, I'll leave that for you to ponder.
The decision is always yours
And yours alone to decide.

When is a Feminine not a Feminine?

To require Feminines to have a logical mind
Requires them to deny their femininity.

To call emotions 'emotional'
in a rather disparaging way
Is ridiculing what makes a Feminine feminine.
It is denying their strengths
By putting them down.

A Feminine by nature is intuitive
They can easily tap into their emotions.
Their particular skill is just knowing the truth
Without needing the evidence as proof.

But they find they are so often required
To produce such concrete and rational evidence
If they are ever to expect to be believed!

The logical mind is a masculine strength
And for that it should be applauded.
But please don't mistake it
For the ultimate strength
So mistakenly thought of as superior.
A strength that therefore wins hands down
Over emotions any day.

For a Feminine
It's easier to keep a lid on their nature
To hide themselves away.
To wear a mask and act a part
To avoid scaring and triggering
Their masculine partners.

Such is the bias built into our lives.

Woke

Woke or being alert to injustice
Birthed with such good intention.
A yearning for a long overdue
Expansion of the mind
A hopefulness, but for what?

Woke, wokery, a pejorative emphasis.
A distain, a superiority, a ridicule
What twaddle is wokeism
Say those who disagree with it.

Why the need to belittle, to crush, to annihilate?
Is it fear that long-held beliefs
Might actually require review?
Is it old power bases feeling foundations
So long established
Shifting so uncomfortably underfoot?
No, this cannot be allowed
It must be strangled at birth
Let's shame it, deny its relevance
That has worked so well before!

But those times, when shaming worked, are gone
The times really are truly changing.
Perhaps, dare I say
Becoming less exclusive
And much more all-encompassing.

So, resist the need to destroy.
Agree to disagree by all means.
But at least have respect and have that debate
With a fully open mind first.
Perhaps some might find themselves
Being genuinely curious
Letting go of that long-held comfort blanket
That has stayed so firmly affixed over the ears.
Others will be reaffirmed in their long-held beliefs
No need to change
To alter what, for them, works so well.
No need to acknowledge that we are not all alike
That what works for them fails so, so miserably
For many, many others.

In truth a person will only change
When they, personally, see a need for change.
That requires us to walk in someone else's shoes
To see through another's eyes
Which is not an easy thing to do.

In the end, the choice is always yours to make.
But next time
If you are tempted to use that word 'woke'
So sneeringly, so pejoratively, so disrespectfully
Pause a moment and ask yourself 'Why?'.

Complacency

We have come a long way!
We have addressed so many inequalities
We should be proud of our progress.
But within that recognition of success
Is a seed of failure
The failure to acknowledge that
There is so much more to do.

Low hanging fruit, glaring inequalities
Have been successfully addressed.
But there is the less obvious
The so well entrenched, that remains unnoticed
By all of us, I might add.
There is a growing risk of an attitude of
'Why are you still dissatisfied?
So many changes have been made in your favour
And you still want more?'
Well, 'in your favour' needs to be challenged
It is a rebalance, not a tipping in anyone's favour.
And as for wanting more, yes, we do!

It takes time and patience and perseverance
But the scales still need rebalancing.
There are those who raise awareness
Be curious and read their work
Then do what you can.

Are you a decision maker? Review your decisions.
If not, be an advocate for change.
But remember, be kind
Rebalancing is not easy for those
Who have been so advantaged in the past.

Do not look for favouritism, it is not called for
Do look for balance.
Good luck, we will all benefit… ultimately!

Double Standards

Anger in a Feminine is unseemly
Showing emotions in a Feminine is a weakness.
How, then, are feminine emotions
To be expressed in such a way
That is deemed, by all, to be acceptable?

If frustration bursts out in tears
It is ridiculed and dismissed.
If frustration bursts out in anger, it is not
Unless it is anger expressed by a Feminine.

Why, I wonder, is anger deemed more acceptable
If it is not a Feminine who is feeling that anger?
All can feel anger
But, it seems, only some may express it.

Evidence

Evidence and proof
Concrete, undeniable facts.
Statistics, averages, probabilities
All essential you know

But what if I 'know' things?
I just know what is right
I can't prove what I know
But I know that I know.

I am told I am foolish for believing such fantasy
For following my hunches and my so-called intuition.
Okay then laugh, if you must
And deride my decisions
It changes me not a jot.
I know what I know and I am so very rarely wrong
And my choices are mine, so evidence... go hang!

But on the subject of evidence
Is the world still deemed flat
Do statistics always agree?
Or is it that facts become flexible over time
Oh, is that an oxymoron, I wonder?

No, I'll just keep it simple
And I'll just stick with my gut!

Battle of the Sexes

Why do we call it 'the battle of the sexes'
As if never the twain shall meet?

Is it when differences only serve to divide
Triggering a need to win the debate?
Instead of those differences being seen
As complementary
Where synergy is the point.

It does require compromise not battle
A respect for expression of differences.
Being able to shelve the need to fully comprehend
(As if a person can ever fully comprehend another).

Life would be boring if our views
Were not challenged
Wouldn't it?

Housewife

'What is your profession?'
'A housewife you say
You would elevate that to the level of profession?'
Indeed, why not be proud
To take your place in the line-up of worthies.
The world might do better
If more people shared
Your dedication to such a profession!

'A housewife?' Said with derogatory inflection.
It may be the same as a stay-at-home dad
But that sounds much more appealing
Less subservient, much less depleting.

'So, what do you do all day
If you are just a housewife?
Surely you must get bored.'
You wish! So in demand, at others' beck and call
So little time for self, for real pamper time.
It's not a nine-to-five job you see
No time off, not so many days holiday per annum.

Not even family holidays are ever really that
Who was it taking on the extra to organise them?
Who made sure that all reached
That so desirable destination
Complete with necessary luggage?!

If you were to write a job description
It might be more obvious what skills are involved
What sacrifice is required
Of your own time and needs.

Chauffeur, organiser extraordinaire
Troubleshooter, shoulder to cry on
The mender of broken and damaged things.
Disciplinarian, last resort for the whole family
Even their friends, particularly those friends
Who do not have a stay-at-home mum!
Totally dependable, prescient even, problems solved
Before they can take their first breath.
The manager of a well-oiled machine, on duty 24/7.

'What's the training?'
'Oh, on the job, trial and error
Deep end and thrown spring to mind.'
'Long service reward?'
'No.'
Well, I just thought it might be worth asking
Before I'm tempted to actually commit.

And then, and then the real kicker.
Please, never, ever expect recognition.
You must be able to survive on no gratitude
And very few compliments, if any.
Expect to be taken for granted
Then you'll never have cause to be disappointed!

Now, how many applicants might you expect
From that particular list of requirements?

Of course, there is a way to prove your worth
Radical though it may be.
Walk out, go on strike, be totally unavailable
Not even on the phone!
Take a well-earned rest
And perhaps even, dare I say, indulge yourself.

And when, or if, you decide to return home
Yes, it might be chaos, take a full week to sort out
But your point will be made and as for you
You will have had that so long overdue
And constantly dreamed of time off.
And the final big bonus...
You might even get more bunches of flowers!

To Plan or Not?

That is a very good question indeed!

A Life That Is Less Than

Why do we fear radical change
Why do we strive for predictable outcomes
Why do we stress if life
Has other ideas
Knocking our plans for six?

Taking a risk
Having no plan
Experimenting with the new
So scary for so many of us
Too scary to allow.
Better the devil you know than the devil you don't
Or is that just the easy way out?

The way, dare I say it, to mediocrity
To a life that is good but not great.

So, back we go to the riskier option
The option that terrifies
And yet tantalises.
Oh, if only life was easy, we say!

But maybe the easy life is so much less than
Have you ever considered that?

Stuck

I can't move forward; things need to change!
Until they change, there is nothing I can do.
And so say we all whenever so tempted
By what is the easy way out.

But what if the problem is much closer to home
What if the solution lies on our own doorstep
What if blaming something 'other' is just an excuse
To not face the truth
That it is only we who stand in our way?

We block ourselves for so many reasons
A belief that we'll find that we're really not capable
Or have nothing of value to offer
A belief that something else must indeed occur first
And that something so conveniently
Is not in our gift.
A very big block though, is a deep fear of risk
And an absolute requirement for
An ironclad guarantee
Without which, you know, it just isn't possible
To take that so huge and so very risky leap.

So life just stands still
With us constantly complaining
Our day dreams strangled at birth.
All the 'if onlys' mean the big, brave intentions
Are then both destined and doomed
To live a life just in fantasy never coming to fruition.

So, in order to start to resolve
Our own very intransigent blocks
No 'ifs or buts' are allowed from now on.
Well, that's if we really want to give ourselves chance
To become a someone
Who's strong and quite fearless.

Monkey Mind

Oh! That's a good idea!
Why didn't I think of it before?

Maybe you did
But last time gradually and persistently
The monkey side of your mind took over.
Don't be silly, you can't do that
You're really just not up to it!
It'll make you look daft
By making a fool of you.
What makes you think that
You know what's best
Better than so-and-so knows?

No, far better to shelve that idea
Why risk this lovely safe space
Where you know, so well, what's what?

I know it's a bit boring
I know you feel frustrated
But would you rather take that huge risk
Of putting yourself 'out there'
Exposing yourself to ridicule?

So the monkey mind drones on
Raising the spectre of fears
So it can then placate you and comfort you
And persuade you that the status quo
Is the sensible choice
In fact, it is the only choice for the sensible mind!

Does any of this sound familiar?
Don't worry you are not alone
Everyone and I mean everyone
Has an active monkey mind!

It's just that some have learnt a few tricks
How to gag that monkey
How to affix effective ear plugs
How to tame it and bring it on side.

Everyone's monkey makes a break
For freedom now and again.
But in time, it starts to doze
To relax
To take its eye off the ball
And finally
It lets you go
To just get on with your life
Unhindered, unfettered
And magnificently and totally unlimited.

What Is the Problem?

We use our minds when solving problems
Problems identified by our minds!
Round and round like a snake eating its tail
Our minds kept so busy
Making work for themselves!

So, spending less time looking for problems
Means less time is spent having to solve them!
Like magic, we have more time on our hands
Time for less stressful, more enjoyable things.

But, our mind says
Order would be in danger of collapse
If problems weren't sufficiently dealt with
Weren't even being identified
Or that they were, and were simply being ignored.

But what if our mind's idea of order
Is, actually, in fact, just way too rigid?
What if we could just let life flow a bit more?
Detach, stop needing to control every last detail
Stop always anticipating problems ahead
Antennae on alert!

Even to stop calling a problem, a problem
So changing completely our attitude towards them.
So many of our so-called problems
Might then be reconsidered
If we were to ask ourselves
Whether just perhaps
That particular something is not meant to be?

Stop forcing, stop requiring
That this or that happens
Then see what transpires, you might be surprised.

Life is so easy if we just let it happen
It is we who make it so hard
It is we who create our own list of problems.

So, what is the problem?
It is us!

What! You Don't Have a Plan?

To live a life without planning
Requires a total rewiring of the brain!
No designated goals
No timescales for achievements
No measures of success and failure.

Instead, it requires an enhanced ability
To recognise signs of wonderful opportunity
And to only pick those that really excite you
However far out they may be
According to your rational mind.

It requires overcoming any feelings of doubt
Any belief that you can't make something succeed.
It requires you to believe
You are worthy of greatness
And of a life that rewards you every day.
It requires you to disconnect from your past
To believe you may not be that person anymore.
It requires you to take it one step at a time
With no obvious direction in mind.

Then it requires you to go out into a world
Seen through the eyes of a child
Where your options are many
And just as importantly
You have all the abilities to cope.

Does it all sound too good to be true?
Well, keep reading this verse over and over
Until the message really sinks in.
I do not say it is easy to change
The habits of a lifetime
And some brains take longer than others
To forge such new behaviours
That truly allow your life to flow.

Money & Possessions

Money and possessions preoccupy the mind
Take up so much of our time
In troubleshooting and organising
Creating distractions from other
More enjoyable things.

Less time for friends, fun things
Relaxation and peaceful existence
All the things that are compromised
By the trappings of wealth
Of success in a worldly sense.

Life passing us by as we
Struggle to get to grips
With controlling our money, our possessions.

So, is it worth it in the end?
We certainly need enough money
To allow us some respite
From making it, from upkeeping
All we buy with it
From searching for and choosing
What to spend it on.

What do we choose to do with such respite?
Relax, socialise, all the things
We don't have time for and miss out on
In our unrelenting pursuit
Of more money and more possessions?

Have we become so engrossed
With the making of money
And the acquisition of possessions
That we might inadvertently risk
Missing the whole point in life?

The Battle of My Heart & Mind

(A very human dilemma)

It's the middle of the night, 2.37am to be precise
The word 'spontaneity' erupts into my head
Quickly followed by a verse
Demanding to be written.

'Where did that come from?
What's it about?'
And there's the dilemma
Made clear in a trice.

My heart says, 'Just write'
My mind says, 'No way!
Let's question the purpose
Don't get carried away.'
The words want to push such questions aside
No judgment, no edit, it's raw and it's fine.
So, let's get on
And if it means I'm nocturnal, then that's okay
When the cat naps tomorrow
Well, I know what to do!

'But I do like control'
Says my mind holding tight
'Nights are for sleep so please do go away.'

My mind wants feelings back in their box
Life has a rhythm, why risk a bodged note?
My mind criticises raw
Because it lacks a fine finish
Must test and review
To deliver the best it can do.

My heart says 'Please don't, I just want to flow
I don't need more discipline
And judgments, you know.'
Self-judgment is harsh and what does it do
But limit and strangle any hopes of the new?
The truly exciting is borne through such rawness
From risking exposure, by allowing the flow.

'If you only do what you've always done
You will only get what you've always got.'
'So please, mind, explain
How do you plan on breaking the mould?'

'But, heart, what needs breaking
When I know exactly what works
It's predictable maybe but what's wrong with that?
Leave me to edit, to check, to be disciplined
Don't force me to change
And put you, heart, on the line.'

And so it goes on, this repetitive battle
Of my heart and my mind.

But what happened to me
When my heart found a way
And the flow became such
That my mind couldn't keep it at bay?
Well, all I can say is, I woke up one morning
And by the end of that day
I had found I was losing my need to control.
Was I worried?
Well, no and I have to concede
That perhaps the controller I thought I was
Just wasn't me!

So, have I found me or lost me
By letting my heart flow so freely?
My mind still says 'Lost!'
My heart says 'Let go!'
So, is this my raw or did my mind get its way?
Well, I must have some secrets
So, I'm not going to say!

Effort & Effortlessness

It is a fine line between effort and effortlessness.
Plans made, dreams concocted, intentions set.
What could possibly go wrong?
Plenty, it seems!
Such hard graft and still it doesn't work
Must try harder, failure is not an option!
Back to the drawing board
Let's call it experience rather than failure.

Stop pushing
See what happens
Same intention but hold it loosely
Go with the flow, be ready to redirect.

Take the blinkers off
Notice luck in all its forms
And how effortless it can be.

Planning Can Lead You Astray!

Are you a meticulous planner
Are you ambitious to reach a set goal
So determined to be undeterred?

But what if you self-censure your own capabilities
Your goals plucked out of a limited pool
What if you believe
You are so much less than you are
Self-assessment clouded
By self-criticism and self-judgment?

Then, the goals that you set
Will never explore your potential
As you ignore and dismiss that
Which you believe to be beyond you.

How will you ever discover your true worth
If you constantly listen to that voice in your head
That says 'No, you can't; you're not up to that!'
And encourages you
To set your goals and plans accordingly.

You may even be the sort of person
Who is able to get on in the world
Being recognised and valued and lauded.
But have you ever stopped to think
'Is this really the best I can do?'

What I Have Learnt

through life's ups and downs

Peace & Contentment

Peace and contentment
Why do they elude so many of us
Why do we struggle to find them?
Is it because we don't allow them into our lives?
They are there if only we could recognise them.

Our needs keep us striving
Our dissatisfaction keeps us looking for more
No wonder so few of us
Find peace and contentment.

It takes a shift of focus
To see what we have already got, already achieved
Not to keep seeing only what we have not got.

Therein lies the secret of peace and contentment
And therein lies the difficulty.

Iceberg

What if the you you see is just
The tip of the iceberg?

What if you have yet to discover your depths
What if you are far more vast
Than you realise
Being so tied up and distracted
By that sparkling top
The small bit that you can easily see
No effort required?

What a waste that would be!

Very Good Friends

What would life be without very good friends?
Lonelier, less meaningful
A much more serious business?

Friends are there when you need them
They laugh with you
They cry with you
They make sure you keep life in perspective.
They help you get over yourself
Boost your confidence when necessary
Give sound advice
But only when you ask for it.

They forgive you
They don't preach
They make allowances
And never say 'I told you so!'

Life would be so much less
In the absence of friends
They are worth the effort
They are
Well, let's just say
As essential as breathing!
And leave it at that.

A Gem of a Life

What thoughts cross your mind when asked
'What are you waiting for?'

Oh, I'll be alright
When so-and-so does this and so-and-so says that
They apologise, come back, take some notice of me
When I can buy this, when I can afford that
When finally this, oh and that too
Is properly sorted out.
And of course, when I find
Absolutely
My best course of action.

In other words
When things are just falling into place
According to my own grand plan.

Until then I shall wait, as patiently as possible
And try not to get
Overwhelmed with frustration.

I shall fill my time
I shall envy those who already have what I want
And then
Well, and, and then…

Hum, but is that really the best way to live
To put life on hold
Make the best of a bad job
Just until things get better, you say?

What if this is it?
The best it can get
Just waiting for you to see it's true value
That life is worth living today, yes today
Right in the everyday now.

Maybe a change of focus might be required
From what you have not got to what you have got
Then you can enjoy the real here and now
Letting tomorrow take care of itself.

Stressing and yearning changes nothing in future
Truly not a single jot
But stressing and yearning can cause you to miss
The gem of a life that is already yours
A life ready made and 'in the bag' so to speak.

So, may I ask you once more
'What is it that you are waiting for?'

Tolerance

Judgment requires some level of perfection
A level that has or has not been achieved.
Criticism depends on a perception of failure
A sense of not quite making the mark.

But what if perfection is a personal value
A value that is not shared by all?
What if failure exists only in some eyes
But in another's is actually quite good enough?

What grief do we cause by constantly measuring
Those that we meet on the way?
What purpose does such grief serve in the long run
Apart from causing unnecessary woe?
Do we really want to be seen as
That overly opinionated, grumpy person
Who just isn't worth getting to know?

The truth of the matter is that one man's perfection
Is a total anathema to others.
Perception is all but then what you perceive
Is very much influenced by the nature
Of your life so far.

So, why waste your time, why not save lots of grief
By letting others just get on with their lives?
Do you really need to feel that you are superior
Because you've got the monopoly on truth?
But you know, it does take all sorts of truths
To make up this, our wide, wonderful world.

Why not simply be curious as to how others tick
To glory in not fearing our differences?
What new can we learn if we never make friends
With those whose views are so different from ours?

Choices & the Risk of Mistakes

Choices, which way to go?
Big or small, some choices are scary
And powerfully life-changing.

It is easy to say when the choice is not clear
'Well, your guess is as good as mine.'
And even to ask 'What do you think I should do?'
Believing that others know better than you.
So, does that mean another's guess
Is to be considered as good as your own
Or indeed, the far better bet?
Well, I have learnt that it's prudent to ask
How can that really be so?
I've learnt that others' choices that should be for me
Only really hold true for them.
It is simply what they believe they would decide
If they were to be in my shoes.
But they are not in my shoes and never can be
So, their choice is fundamentally flawed
I've learnt that I delegate my choice at my peril.
Even whilst hoping for the best.

I might keep others happy
By following their guidance
But what is the price I have paid?

To ensure my best life, I must choose for myself
Or, run the risk of remorse and regret.
Please believe me when I do say that these
Are too big a price to pay.
My hard-won choices may meet with derision
May even be judged as quite mad!
But if a choice feels right and makes my heart sing
If it solves my frustrations and anxieties of today
Then I ignore the naysayers
Because it's my life, not theirs.

And if I make a mistake and am most gleefully told
'What did I tell you? Why didn't you listen?'
Well, I am only human and therefore not perfect
So, I'll not be put off by the chances of that!
If I must own mistakes
Then better that they're mine
Far better than living with the mistakes
Caused by others!

The secret is out, we all make mistakes
Even those who might like to claim
That, as they know best, we should follow their lead
If we want to avoid a mistake!

As no-one is better or worse than me
When it comes to making mistakes
I'll make my own choices and risk my mistakes
I'm worth it and so too are you.

What Do I Want?

I want the world to be more loving
More tolerant and more just.

A happier place to live.

But to be more just requires more tolerance
To be more tolerant requires more love
And so, there it is!
How easy and yet oh so hard!

I don't give up hope
We are all capable of more love
We just have to be willing to try.

It

If you never have a lack of it
You will never experience full appreciation of it
Whatever 'it' might be!
Anticipation, missing it, hoping for it
Aspirations, aims, planning for it
All are part of the full experience of it
The absence of any detracts, even destroys
The ultimate pleasure in it.
Overindulgence kills desire for it
Where is the hungry desire for something
You have too much of already?
Desire is what makes life worth living.

So, don't wish the quality of your life away
By wishing you had it all already
You don't know what you risk losing
If desire is no longer at play in your life.

Labels

We are constantly asked to label ourselves
What do we call ourselves?
What religion?
What nationality?
What job?
What are our politics?
And in each and every case
Our answers
Set ourselves up to be misunderstood.

What we mean when we use a label
Is by no means necessarily
What another interprets that label to mean.
If we seek to misdirect
All well and good
If we mean to enlighten
It's not so good!

Labels are oversimplifications anyway
So, why do we ask for them?
To keep life simple?
If so, we will fail more often than not
As the wrong end of the stick is grasped
And complicates matters
So much more so!

Beware of the Unaware Question!

'How do you feel about that?'
What an unaware question to ask.
When has anyone ever been able
To communicate how they feel
To another using words?
It is impossible
And, if you don't understand that
You don't understand feelings!
You are trying to intellectualise a feeling
Which, in truth, cannot be done!
We don't say 'actions speak louder than words'
Without very good reason indeed.

Feelings defy words, they are felt
They are, though, very real
And they may indeed influence what is said.

But what is said
Will not be describing the feelings themselves
Only the thoughts associated with them.
The mind's feeble attempts to rationalise them
To reduce feelings to a mind-based concept
Explicable in words.

So never ask another
'How do you feel about that?'
Unless you want to show your ignorance
About feelings of course!

Getting to Know You

A stranger.
Polite introductions
'Hello, how are you, lovely day, isn't it?
So, what do you do?'
And there we have it!
Straight to the point.
Not 'Who are you?' No, too vague and too revealing
Risk of too much information.
No, safer to ask 'What do you do?'
Actually, it's more useful, isn't it?
It answers the questions:
How important are you?
How clever?
How worth knowing or not?
Is this conversation going to be worth my while?
Are we likely to have anything much in common?
All far more questionable
Therefore unspoken motives
Most probably totally unacknowledged, in truth.

We think we are getting to know someone
But are we really?
What does the answer to that question
Actually tell us?

It tells us about a person's role in life, that's all.
It gives us clues, but only clues
About how much they are likely to be worth.
It lets us attempt to peg them into place
On some sort of social scale
As if that might be important to us.

Such conclusions we jump to, some right
And others, most certainly, very, very wrong
Judgments and misjudgments both.
It tells us nothing about who they actually are
What makes them tick?
Are they happy or sad?
Are they fulfilled or rather frustrated?
Assuming of course
That we might be the slightest bit interested
In any of that crap…
As some might so charmingly put it!

At best
It only tells us what they have done in the past
At least the bits they are willing to admit to
It behoves us to remember
That they have already calculated
What is likely to make them look good in our eyes
To be truthful
But only to a point!

'So, nothing about who they are then?'
'No.'

What's more now, right now
We are, none of us
Even our past, if truth were told
It is called our past because it is past
It is no longer!

So, how useful is the question
'What do you do?'
When the question requires and the answer provides
Simply information about a role in life
Just the mask
Behind which each of us truly exists?

I'll leave that for you to decide.

Exploring Our Dark Side

Fears, doubts, shame and guilt

Feelings

Feelings
So belittled
So chastised
In a world of power, competitiveness
Goals and aspirations
Where can they reside?

Undeveloped, unacknowledged
Ultimately totally unfelt
Still existing but buried, so, so deep
Benefits lost
World gone astray.

No-one seems to feel.
We all do, but have lost the ability
To express, emote, expose our deeper selves
For fear of shame and ridicule.

Freedom of Choice

It is not necessary for another to limit our choices
We easily limit them ourselves, whilst still believing
We are exercising our very own free will!

It is easy to see when another person limits us.
The far harder limits to spot and with which to deal
Are the ones we impose upon ourselves
The ones that remain unacknowledged
Unrecognised, unchallenged
And so very, very unuseful.

But surely if it is our choice, unlimited by others
That means we are exercising our own free will?

Yes, but we are not necessarily
Allowing ourselves full freedom of choice.

If we recognise that it is
Some fear, guilt or shame within us
That is driving us to limit our choices
And still we make that limited choice
Despite full knowledge of what is driving it
Then we have undoubtably exercised
Free will in making that choice.
A choice to limit our freedom of choice.

But we might not realise that such is the case
When we do something because
We should or we ought to
If we choose out of a sense of having to
As if no other choice is available to us
If we are to be able to live with ourselves.
Though we know that choice
Will not enhance our lives or make us feel good.

It is then that we need to acknowledge
That our fears are getting the better of us
That it is our fears that prevent us
From considering all options
And that we are therefore self-sabotaging
Our freedom of choice
Our happiness
And perhaps even ultimately
Our wellbeing too.

Superficial

We all do it!
Those superficial judgments on first meeting
Thinking we know someone well enough
To dismiss them, to explore them no further.

But then, what riches might we be
Excluding from our lives?
And why do we do it so readily?

Are we afraid of what we might find
If we were to dig a bit deeper, to be more curious?
Do we fear finding that, yes, they are different
That we might have to change a something in us
In order to successfully accommodate them?

Do we risk upsetting our well-organised lives
Our opinions of what is acceptable?

Or is it rather simpler than that
Are we just fearing that we are inferior
Or maybe believing that they are beneath us
That we are, in fact, superior to them?

Whatever the reason we instantly judge
A person as someone worth knowing or not
It is that reason that bears some reflection
As it tells us a something quite valuable about us.
Indeed, it reveals more about us
Than it ever can do about them.

Giving & Taking

They say to give is a kindness, a virtue.
As every single giving requires
By necessity, a taking
Is that a virtue too?

To answer that I find I must question
Both the giving and the taking.

Why are we giving?
In truth, the reasons may be light or dark.

Are we giving without an expectation
Of getting something back
With a generous spirit and out of kindness?
Such giving is easy to define as a virtue.

Or, do we give because we need to give
To justify our existence, to make us feel worthy
To make us feel acceptable to others
To assuage some sense of guilt
Some sense of being responsible
For another's wellbeing, their happiness?
Hum, those reasons might be trickier
To justify as a virtue.

Do we give so that the taker
Whoever they may be
Becomes indebted, owing us
Giving us the upper hand in our
Future relationship with them?
Or giving us a bone fide reason
To complain about them later
If they are not equally generous back?
No need to say this sort of giving
Makes the world a darker place to live.

Then, of course, there is the taking.
An open-hearted giver wants us to take.
But there are those who absolutely require us to take
Taking offence, feeling slighted, if we don't.

Open-hearted giving is most definitely
Something to accept, graciously, thankfully
That is the virtuous choice.
How would you feel if your gift was put aside
Even refused outright?
Perhaps though, we sense there is a hidden agenda
So we may end up taking, to avoid repercussion.
This, of course, is not so good.

Then there is the habitual giving and taking.
An expectation, on both sides
Built up over years, decades perhaps
When the giver keeps giving and giving and giving
Far beyond any reasonable degree of giving.
The taker, whose expectations
Far from being assuaged
Grow and expand, encouraging the taker
To keep on taking and taking, never giving in return.
Stuck in a rut.   Both parties.
Needless to say, all this is really not so good.

It is always worth remembering
When it comes to giving and taking
That no-one is ever responsible for another
All other things being equal of course.
A person may be in difficulty
But it is, in truth, their difficulty and theirs to solve
Help, yes but never, ever feel responsible for them.

So, I always find it worth asking myself
Why do I want to give or to take?
Do I really, really want to give or take?
It's a very revealing test!

Fear

It matters not how beautiful the prison
A prison is a prison, real or imagined.

Our minds can trap us in ever-decreasing circles
Desperate for a way out
But walking past the open door
Over and over again.

Others cannot fathom our blindness
To that wide-open door
We are bright, intelligent
Why can't we see it?

Our fear veils our eyes
Blurs what should be crystal clear
Hinders our lives, our joys, our peace of mind.

So, is it time to just stand still
Raise our hands and start to lift
The corner of that veil?
Just a tiny bit at first lest we are blinded
By the brightness of the world
Waiting for us.

Take time, enough time as you need
That beautiful, bright world
Will wait patiently for us.

Is It Me or Is It Them?

The art of projection.
Believing and broadcasting this or that about them
When really we are describing us
And just calling it them!

Why do we do it?
Because it's our dark side
The side we don't want to accept
Because if we did, we might have to face
The need to do something about it.

It's so much easier to blame someone else
To make it their problem.
We can even stand proud
Draw attention to their failings
Criticise and feel superior
Making ourselves look so much better than them.

No matter that we describe ourselves
Oh so accurately
Whilst believing we are talking about them.

No matter that it is just that we cannot admit
That really it is all about us.

Justice

It is easy to get justice for the wholly undeserving
When a system is skewed in their favour.
When there is blindness to equity
At times even wilful
What hope is there that justice
Can be available to all?

So many systems require
A deep and thoroughly forensic overhaul
But that requires those who won't take time to see
To be honest and admit that it's too easy to keep
Heads under the parapet, to not rock the boat
Or risk making an enemy
Of those who grow rich
On maintaining the rotten and abusive status quo.

Good Enough

We are all good enough!

Even those who cannot see it
Whose minds, egos and fears get in the way.

Even those who want to belittle us
To make us feel small
But who only need to bolster
Their own very fragile sense of worth.

And even those who strive to prove themselves
The very best, the greatest
Those on the hamster wheel of more and more
Bigger and bigger, riskier and riskier
Because to be less so would make them feel
Too vulnerable.

But nothing allays such fears
The real fears behind it all
Of not being good enough
Of not ever having enough
Of not doing it all.

All the money, success or fame in the world
Cannot allay those fears and fill that inner void.
The deep sense that something is lacking
Some sense of having failed
Of being considered unsuccessful
In this game, this game we call life.

If only they all knew
That deep, deep inside
They are really quite good enough.
That they are, indeed, a sufficiently good
A quite lovable, though flawed
Human being.

Coercive Control

Why don't you just leave?
Why do you go along with it
Accept the unacceptable
Excuse such bad behaviour
Hide the hurt, keep smiling through it?

Is it because you can't believe
That the one you trust
Have built your life with, are loyal to
Is actually undeserving of that trust, that loyalty?
Do you just want to ignore how bad it is?
Do you feel that you deserve to be treated badly
That you only have yourself to blame?
Are your lives so inextricably linked
That leaving is no easy task?
Joint assets, joint accounts
So little that is solely yours if you leave.
Negotiations needed but impossible to have
No plans made in case things should go awry
No safeguards put in place.

Walking on eggshells day in, day out.
Then there is the gaslighting
The projections of inadequacy
The belittling constantly
All from the person you believe
You can trust the most.

You think you are good
That you are so capable
But they say not, again and again and again.
Perhaps they are right and you are just so wrong?
Maybe you don't know yourself like they do
Maybe you should feel ashamed
Maybe it is your fault when things go wrong
As they so often do, more often than not.

Then, like sunshine breaking through clouds
A moment of kindness, of apparent thoughtfulness
You matter, you are the best thing
That ever happened to them!

It lasts just long enough
To make you doubt your doubts.
They need you
They are the poor victim of circumstances
They deserve your care and protection.

Then it begins again, down the rabbit hole.
You don't work hard enough
You don't pull your weight
You are a burden, you should do more, earn more.
A relentless tirade that wears down
The strongest defences.
Shame keeps you silent
Shame and feeling to blame keeps you beholden.

Decades pass. Why do you stay?

Because you believe you are needed
Are doing something good with your life
And you so want to be a good person
Doesn't everyone?

But then, exhaustion.
Spinning in ever-decreasing circles
Until you feel as if you are spinning on the spot
Doing nothing, going nowhere
No future, no respite in sight.
What could possibly be worse?
Got to get out, get away from all this.

Then, openly and oh so bravely expressing
A desire to leave in a last-ditch attempt
To finally provoke that long overdue conversation
To salvage something, change something
Anything.

The vice turns tighter.
The silent treatment, no hoped-for conversation.
The distain. The ridicule
'You think you can leave me?
You're a fantasist, you can't manage without me.'
More punishment, withdrawal of basic requirements.

The veil starts to lift
The ugly truth starts to be revealed
Try to excuse it
But your mind reluctantly has to see
Just what it is that has stayed hidden
That you've denied for so long.

You finally leave, plans executed efficiently
You realise you are capable
You are able to do things without them
Indeed it is far, far easier without
That monstrous blockage
So intent on preventing change.

Then, more eye-opening, the vindictiveness
The spreading of slander about you.
The law capable of making you homeless
Because it does not understand that you are
Still brainwashed, exhausted, vulnerable.
That they, the law, are being cleverly manipulated
Into prolonging the control.
Not understanding that what is said
Is not what will happen.
Promises broken, time scales extended indefinitely.
You can't blame the law
Weren't you duped for far longer
And to a much greater extent?

A coercive controller is clever, charming
Projecting their bad behaviour onto the abused.
Are so, so plausible and therefore believed
They are the victim
The one who deserves the law's protection.

Eventually, you come out the other side
Free, independent, alone but happy.
Wiser, poorer, the law doesn't recognise 50:50
Even after three decades of marriage
But perversely, feeling richer
As money is far, far from everything
Because even a wealthy prison is still a prison.

Rehabilitation takes time
Trust in others takes even longer.
Joy and laughter and happiness though
Make even that bad, bad interminable nightmare
Of leaving, breaking the ties
So very, very worthwhile.

The Power of the Law

The law now recognises coercive control.
The law of precedent says not!

What use are fine intentions
When clever brains duck and dive
Quote this case and that case
Blind you with precedent
Which is theirs to know
And for you to remain forever fazed.

Trusting the might of the law will protect you
You discover that making yourself homeless
For eighteen long, long months
Is actually preferable
To the impossible alternative on offer.
No-one recognises your dilemma.
It's your choice, what can they do?
But you know the punishment
Just waiting to pounce
For having had the insolence
The audacity to leave.

Homelessness or more, much more imprisonment
With a merciless controller
So clever, so charming, so manipulative
So totally concealed from the public eye.
The virtuous victim if they are to be believed.
They are believed.

But then, that's the nature of coercive control
With its gaslighting weaponry and skills
It's sneaky and deadly and impossible to prove.
And, of course, all must be afforded
The benefit of the doubt
This is justice after all
We must take care to be fair!

So, so much so for trust, that's a laugh!
But better laugh than cry
Yourself to sleep every night
You learn to laugh
The hard way.

You find out who your friends really are
They can be trusted
Are worth their weight in gold
Thank God.

Why are we surprised?
The law can't change just like that
Even when the words sound so fine and hopeful.

Old habits die hard
Complexity is built in
Case law going back to times when power was all
He who had it won.

Coercive control was used to win
Though of course, God forbid
Anyone might dare to call it that!

We must continue to live in hope
That the death throes of such an archaic system
Are not too prolonged
And that fresh, fresh air can be allowed to cleanse
And restore our justice.

But then
That depends where the power lies.

A New Way of Living

Reminders of what makes life easier

The Secret of Happiness

Some are just born lucky!

But most have dug deep
Faced many inner fears
And conquered them all.

They are happy despite all the odds.

Don't Worry

When did worry ever change the outcome?
When is worry ever
A necessary part of life?

So, why do we feel so compelled to worry
To expect that the worst will happen?
Such expectations requiring us
To plan ahead so we are fully
And completely prepared.

How much time we waste
How much stress we cause ourselves
By our 'what ifs' and 'buts'
When the worst
Simply fails to materialise.

We won't get that time back again!

Your Life

Are you living your life
Or do you put another's needs before your own?
Would you expect that other
To put your needs before their own?
If you answer yes and then no
Perhaps it's time to reflect
To ask yourself why you feel so unworthy
To the point of making your personal contentment
So assuredly out of reach.

It is not generosity of spirit
If it means you must devalue yourself in the process
By rating another as more important than you.

That is a mistake so many of us make
Before we find ourselves wondering why
We have to suffer such consequences.

Approval

What might others think
Will they approve?
More importantly, will they judge me as wanting?
How many times do we ask ourselves
Those questions?
How many times do we inhibit our natural desires
In case we might meet with disapproval
Be judged unfavourably by others?

It is so easy to become what we are not by nature
As we attempt to please others
To win approval
To be thought of as good.
And all the time, we deny who we really are
We labour under the illusion we create
We go through the motions
To live a life that is not our life to live.

Our lives are lives
That make us leap out of bed in the morning
In anticipation of a wonderful day ahead.

Can you give yourself even a glimpse
Of what that life could be like?
Can you wean yourself off the need for approval
Be a bit of a rebel
And live your life
Not the life required of you by others?

It does require you to give yourself permission
To go there.
Don't keep waiting for others to tell you it's okay
They won't
Because they can't read your heart
Only you can do that.

Analysis

Wallowing in our woes
Analysing, digging, focusing
Trying to understand why me?
Who is responsible?
What caused it?

No, stop there!
Stop trying to fathom the unfathomable.
When there appear to be no accessible answers
Move on from the past.
Our past does not dictate our future anyway
Unless we let it.

If only we could all have collective amnesia
Become as innocent and naïve as children
Play a little, dream a little
The world might be a better place.

That Little Voice Inside Our Head

We don't need others to beat us up
We do a very good job of it ourselves!
The standards we set
The height of the bar
It is that that ensures our defeat.

Others may wonder what the fuss is about
They see our strength
They see how valiantly we strive
They wonder at our resilience.

On the subject of criticism they are silent.
It is only our minds
That clamour for attention.
It is only our minds
That won't let us forget
Our so-called failures and deficiencies.

Day Dreaming Into Life

They say we are the authors
Of our own particular destiny.
So, do you create a life
Of harmony or discord?
Apparently, it is up to us
We are in charge, so to speak!

If we truly manifest what we think about most
Whatever we concentrate our minds upon
Is it a wonder that so many of us
Will end up so dissatisfied with life!

Reflect upon your mental ruminations today
What one single thought
Has dominated your mind?
Would that be what you would welcome
If it came into your life?
Or, do you really, really want
The complete, exact opposite
Having spent the day worrying and anxious
And even perhaps feeling fearful?

If our thoughts really do dictate our future
Are you on track to create your best life
Or your complete and total worst nightmare?

So, if for the next twenty-four hours
We focus on our wildest, most desirable dreams
I certainly can't promise instant success
But I can assure you that you will be having
A much more enjoyable twenty-four hours!

And, repeat that habit every twenty-four hours
And then perhaps, just perhaps
Your life will transform to become a life
That is very much more worth living.

Safe Space

Do not apologise or berate yourself
For failing some self-imposed
Test of perfection.

Instead, be proud of your ability
To express your imperfections to others.

We are our imperfections
As well as our perfections.
But we spend so much time and energy
Hiding them from the world
Ashamed of our very selves
Denying who we are to ourselves
As well as to others.
Ever watchful, lest the mask slips
And reveals our dark side.

But when we do express our true selves
What a surprise is in store!
Others heave a sigh of relief
Maybe only silently.

The overwhelming requirement
To always be perfect
Has been lifted
By the brave soul
Who has expressed their dark side
And just put it out there.

Loud and proud!

Energy

Energy, around us, within us, connecting us
Dividing us.
We are energetic beings
Obsessed with the tangible, physical body
Its ailments, its looks, its ageing
Such obsessions blind us to our true magnificence.

The physical body is just a fraction of our selves.
Our logical, rational minds limit us
To believe only that that can be proved
Be seen, be touched, be tested.

But what constitutes proof?
What if the nature of that in itself
Is limited by our minds?

Absence of evidence is not evidence of absence.
To go beyond, we must go beyond the mind
And its rational thinking.
'Ridiculous' say some, 'bring it on' say others.
Which camp do you fall into?

So, let's accept for a moment
That our energy extends far beyond our outer skin
That it blends and merges with the energy
Of everything and everyone around us
It connects us irrevocably to the Universe
The Cosmos, to Entirety
A great big, pulsing, living, exciting, energetic Union
Impossible to draw the line where we stop
And the rest begins.

A room of people becomes a room
Packed full of swirling, interacting, blended energies
That feels safe for some and threatening to others.
Why is clashing, demanding, pushy, punchy energy
Exhilarating for some
And so exhausting and draining for others?
Unless we go beyond and explore
Our energetic selves, those answers remain elusive.
We do not fully navigate relationships, situations
If we fail to acknowledge and read the energy
The subtle interactions
We participate in so unwittingly.
Do we bombard others simply by our presence
Or disappear even when in plain sight?
Are we inviting the wrong people in
Without realising it
Or unknowingly pushing the right people away?

So, explore, enquire, feel your way into your energy
We all have it!
A whole new, wonderful, bigger, wider world
Is beckoning to us
If we can put our rational minds aside
Just for a moment.

Being Human

To err is to be human
You must never deny yourself that.

Perfection is impossible.
What a shame
Such a word even exists
To taunt us and condemn us.

About the Author

I had intended to describe the life experiences that led me to writing this book of verse. However, I realised this wasn't necessary.

Why?

Because who I was is not who I am now, nor who I will be in the future. I realised my past is irrelevant, apart from what I have learnt from it, and that is already recorded in the preceding pages.

Acknowledgements

My acknowledgements must include everyone I have ever known as my interactions, both good and bad with family, friends and acquaintances, have all contributed to the gradual process of exploration that has led me to change my attitude and become a far happier me.

Some have offered help and care of great value. I hope I have been able to express my gratitude at the time and that they therefore know who they are. To them particularly, once again, I say thank you from the bottom of my heart; you are worth your weight in gold.

Index

A Gem of a Life   72

A Life That is Less Than   49

Analysis   118

An Idea of Me   20

Approval   116

Battle of the Sexes   42

Being Human   127

Beware of the Unaware Question!   81

Choices & the Risk of Mistakes   76

Coercive Control   102

Complacency   38

Day Dreaming Into Life   120

Don't Worry   114

Double Standards   40

Effort & Effortlessness   63

Energy   124

Equity   32

Evidence   41

Fear   97

Freedom of Choice   90

Feelings   89

Getting to Know You   82

Giving & Taking   94

Good Enough   100

Housewife   43

Iceberg   70

I Don't Really Like You!   15
I Have a Question   29
Is It Me or Is It Them?   98
It   79
I Will Never Be a Feminist!   30
Justice   99
Labels   80
Longing   17
Love & Loss   16
Loss   14
Loyalty   25
Mistaken Identity   22
Money & Possessions   58
Monkey Mind   52
Peace & Contentment   69
Planning Can Lead You Astray!   64
Player   18
Safe Space   122
Superficial   92
Stuck   50
That Little Voice Inside Our Head   119
The Battle of My Heart & Mind   60
The Power of the Law   107
The Secret of Happiness   113
The Very Best Gift   13
Tolerance   74
Touch   21
Very Good Friends   71
What Do I Want?   78
What Is the Problem?   54

What! You Don't Have a Plan?   56
When is a Feminine not a Feminine?   34
Woke   36
Your Life   115

Milton Keynes UK
Ingram Content Group UK Ltd.
UKHW040640041023
429927UK00004B/125